CLASSIC CARS
1931·1980

NORM MORT

x1000r/min

CRABTREE PUBLISHING COMPANY
www.crabtreebooks.com

Crabtree Publishing Company

www.crabtreebooks.com

TO MY WIFE SANDY, WHO NEVER COMPLAINS WHEN
YET ANOTHER "CLASSIC" SHOWS UP IN OUR DRIVEWAY.

Coordinating editor: Ellen Rodger
Series Editor: Rachel Eagen
Editors: Adrianna Morganelli, Carrie Gleason,
L. Michelle Nielsen, Jennifer Lackey
Design and production coordinator: Rosie Gowsell
Production assistance: Samara Parent
Art direction: Rob MacGregor
Scanning technician: Arlene Arch
Photo research: Allison Napier
Prepress technician: Nancy Johnson

Consultants: Petrina Gentile Zucco, Automotive Journalist,
The Globe and Mail

Photo Credits: Rodolfo Arpia/Alamy: p. 19 (top); Bob Masters Classic
Car Images/Alamy: p. 11 (top); Gary Cook/Alamy: p. 27 (top); Martin
Diver/Alamy: p. 22 (bottom); Andre Jenny/Alamy: p. 28 (bottom); Pep
Roig/Alamy: p. 7 (bottom); Phil Talbot/Alamy: p. 23 (bottom);
wherrett.com/Alamy: p. 26; Colin Woodbridge/Alamy: p. 28 (middle);
Visions of America, LLC/Alamy: p. 31 (bottom); AP/Wide World
Photos: p. 13 (bottom); AP Photos/Lefteris Pitarakis: p. 27 (bottom);

Bettmann/Corbis: p. 8; Richard Cummins/Corbis: p. 29 (bottom); Robert
Dowling/Corbis: p. 30; Courtesy of the Detroit News: p. 13 (top); The
Granger Collection, New York: p. 6, p. 9 (top), p. 15 (bottom); Mary
Evans Picture Library/The Image Works: p. 29 (top); Roger-Viollet/The
Image Works: p. 31 (top); Scherl/SV-Bilderdienst/The Image Works: p. 9
(bottom); Topham/The Image Works: p. 15 (top); Ron Kimball/Ron
Kimball Stock: cover, p. 1, p. 7 (top), p. 10, p. 11 (bottom), p. 12, p. 14,
p. 16, p. 17 (both), p. 18, p. 19 (bottom), p. 20, p. 21 (both), p. 22 (top),
p. 23 (top), p. 25 (both), p. 28 (top); Tom McHugh/Photo Researchers,
Inc.: p. 24.

Cover: This classic 1957 Chevrolet Bel Air convertible is parked
in front of a diner, a classic 1950s hangout.

Title page: Classic car enthusiasts do not only collect cars, such
as this 1964 Volkswagen Karmann Ghia, but also automobilia, or
car memorabilia, including signs from old gas stations and car
part manufacturers.

Library and Archives Canada Cataloguing in Publication

Mort, Norm
    Classic cars, 1931-1980 / Norm Mort.

(Automania!)
Includes index.
ISBN 978-0-7787-3012-5 (bound)
ISBN 978-0-7787-3034-7 (pbk.)

   1. Antique and classic cars--Juvenile literature.
2. Automobiles--History--Juvenile literature. I. Title. II. Series.

TL15.M67 2007   j629.222   C2007-900650-7

Library of Congress Cataloging-in-Publication Data

Mort, Norm.
  Classic cars : 1931-1980 / written by Norm Mort.
    p. cm. -- (Automania!)
  Includes index.
  ISBN-13: 978-0-7787-3012-5 (rlb)
  ISBN-10: 0-7787-3012-3 (rlb)
  ISBN-13: 978-0-7787-3034-7 (pb)
  ISBN-10: 0-7787-3034-4 (pb)
  1. Automobiles--History--Juvenile literature. 2. Antique and classic
cars--Juvenile literature. I. Title. II. Series.

TL15.M66 2007
629.22209--dc22   2007003410

Crabtree Publishing Company

Printed in the USA/201803/HF20180214

www.crabtreebooks.com   1-800-387-7650

**Published in
Canada
Crabtree Publishing**
616 Welland Ave.
St. Catharines, ON
L2M 5V6

**Published in the
United States
Crabtree Publishing**
PMB 59051
350 Fifth Avenue, 59th Floor
New York, New York 10118

**Published in the United
Kingdom
Crabtree Publishing**
Maritime House
Basin Road North, Hove
BN41 1WR

**Published in Australia
Crabtree Publishing**
3 Charles Street
Coburg North
VIC, 3058

CONTENTS

TRIED AND TRUE

Classic cars are older cars that people love to own and drive. Classic cars get noticed on the street because they look different from the modern cars of today. Classic cars have style, and often have interesting touches, such as shiny chrome detailing and bright paint jobs.

A CLASS ABOVE THE REST

There are many different types of classics, but all of them have superior performance or styling that makes them different from other cars that were built around the same time. Customized bodywork and fancy **radiator** ornaments were seen on luxury cars of the 1920s and 1930s, while high-performance engines paired with rigid **suspensions** were common on classic sports cars of the 1960s. Most classics were expensive to purchase at the time they were built, and are much more expensive now that they are **obsolete**.

Some of the most popular classic cars today are convertibles, which have roofs that can be folded back or removed to provide open-air rides. This late 1950s Corvette convertible turned heads with its curved body lines, dual headlights, and shiny chrome detailing. Its whitewall tires show another popular trend of the 1950s. These tires included a stripe of white rubber on the outer side wall.

THE TEST OF TIME

People like classic cars for several reasons. They are pieces of automotive history, and many people are interested in how these old cars were made and driven. Classic cars are also beautiful to look at, especially the ones that have been carefully **restored**. Restored cars are also often worth a lot of money. Some classic car enthusiasts have passions for particular models because they have fond memories from childhood of riding around in the cars their parents or grandparents owned. Other people dream of owning the car they wanted as teenagers, but could not afford.

THE CLASSIC AGE

Classic car enthusiasts do not always agree on when the classic car era began and ended. Most agree that it began around 1931, after the vintage car era ended. Some believe that the classic era was over by 1950, but several models built during the 1950s, 1960s, and 1970s are considered classics among most enthusiasts today.

(above) Classic cars often feature unusual design elements, such as the porthole windows on this 1956 Ford Thunderbird.

(below) Classic car enthusiasts admire models built by British manufacturer Aston Martin.

THE FIRST CLASSICS

Many car collectors love luxury cars that were built from 1925 to 1948. These cars had the best performance, engineering, styling, and luxury features. Only the wealthiest people could afford one of these cars brand new. Few were built and even fewer are around today.

A LUXURY RIDE

The first classic luxury cars were built around 1925. They had powerful engines with four to six, and sometimes as many as 12, **cylinders**, which allowed the cars to achieve high speeds. They also had lavish interiors, with big, soft, comfortable seats and plenty of leg room to stretch out. Some of these cars had footrests, flower vases, cabinets with drinking glasses, and rear window blinds for passengers in the back.

Open luxury cars, or cars without roofs, often had a second windshield to protect back seat passengers from the wind. These large, powerful cars had **custom-built** bodies that were made by coachwork companies. Owners personalized their cars by choosing the type of wood accenting and leather or other cloth they wanted in the interiors of their cars.

A wealthy couple poses beside their luxury vehicle in the early 1930s. At this time, running boards were attached to the bodies of cars. People stepped on the boards to help them get in.

CLASSIC COACHBUILDERS

There were dozens of different coachbuilders in every car manufacturing country in the world at this time. Coachbuilding companies were usually owned by one or two people. They hired stylists to design car bodies, and craftsmen to build them. Wood was used to build most car frames into the 1930s. The wooden frame was often covered in **aluminum** and sheet metal, but sometimes with another type of wood, or even fabric, such as canvas. Coachbuilders then fitted the body of the car onto the chassis, or main body, which came from a car manufacturer. The car was then sent back to the manufacturer, where the engine and other mechanical parts were added. The finished cars were delivered to **showrooms**, for the wealthy to purchase. Some coachbuilt cars could be changed to suit the weather. A stylish, open body with a roof that folded back was used in good weather, while a closed roof was fitted for winter.

The interior of this classic car was built using expensive materials, including wood and leather.

Packards were known for their powerful, 12-cylinder engines, which provided ultra smooth handling.

BLACK TUESDAY

Coachbuilt cars were popular among the wealthy in the early 1920s, but as the decade progressed, cars became affordable to more people, and car manufacturers produced more vehicles to keep up with the demand.

WE'RE IN THE MONEY!

Toward the end of the 1920s, car sales increased as people had more money to spend. Many people began **investing** in companies by buying their **stocks**. Some people even borrowed money to buy more stocks, as they hoped the stocks would become more valuable and they would make a profit. The prices of many stocks increased, and people continued to buy them, confident that they would become wealthy.

CRASH AND BURN

On Tuesday October 29, 1929, stock prices rapidly decreased. People began to panic, and tried to sell their stocks. Since no one was interested in buying worthless stock, many people lost all of their money. Companies went bankrupt as the United States entered the Great Depression. This period marked an economic low point worldwide. Many people lost their jobs and could not find work. No pay check meant families were often hungry. The stock market crash is sometimes referred to as "Black Tuesday."

The Great Depression began in 1929 and lasted for most of the 1930s. Many people were unemployed, left with little money. These people are waiting in line for free food at a soup kitchen.

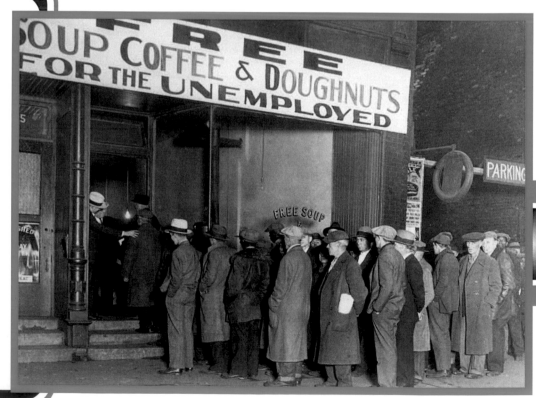

The Chrysler Airflow 1934

The Chrysler Airflow moved away from the boxy designs of the era. The Airflow's rounded edges made the car look more aerodynamic.

LAST OF THE COACHBUILDERS

The Great Depression lasted about ten years. People struggled to pay rent and buy groceries. Cars quickly became luxury items that most people could not afford to buy. Car companies had fewer customers, and many of them went out of business. Coachbuilders became a trend of the past, as even the wealthy had less money to spend, and driving around in fancy cars had less appeal with so many people out of work. Some of the larger coachbuilders held on by producing other items, such as bathroom fixtures. Other coachbuilders were purchased by larger car manufacturers.

People without shelter during the Great Depression were forced to sleep on the floors of public buildings, using newspapers as blankets.

THE THIRTIES

In the 1930s, most people had little money. Despite this, large car manufacturers continued to produce luxury cars. Cadillac, Packard, and Lincoln were among the manufacturers who survived the Great Depression, producing some of the most famous classic cars to date.

THE TEST OF TIME

Throughout the 1930s, dozens of small car manufacturers, such as Stutz, Pierce-Arrow, Cord, Duesenberg, and many others, went out of business. Larger car companies, such as Ford, General Motors, Chrysler, Studebaker, Hudson, Nash, and Packard struggled throughout the decade, but survived.

This roadster was built by Ford in the early 1930s. A roadster is a convertible that usually has only two seats.

THE CLASSIC 1930S

The cars of the 1930s were longer and lower to the ground than cars of the 1920s. Cars from the 1930s had rounded edges, which made them look less boxy. Enclosed cars were more popular than open rides, and many cars came with windows that could be rolled up or down. Car bodies were no longer made of wood and canvas, but were instead made entirely of steel. Gravel roads were paved, which meant that little dust blew up into passengers' eyes. People began traveling greater distances, sometimes even taking overnight trips. Larger trunks were designed into the bodywork of cars.

THE BEAUTIFUL "DUESSIE"

Errett Lobban Cord founded the Cord Corporation in 1929. The company was made up of several companies, including Auburn, Cord, and Duesenberg. The Cord Corporation built some of America's most beautiful cars, including the Duesenberg Model J, one of the most expensive and powerful cars in the world. Only 480 were built between 1929 and 1935. Everyone dreamed of owning a Duesenberg.

Only wealthy people, such as royalty, could afford to buy the Duesenberg Model J.

THE COFFIN NOSE CORD

Errett Lobban Cord introduced a car named after himself in 1929. The Cord was considered a breakthrough because it had front-wheel drive. This meant that the engine powered the front wheels, rather than the rear wheels, as in most cars at this time. A new version of the Cord, the "coffin nose," debuted in 1936. It had hide-away headlamps that disappeared into the front fenders, and a long, narrow, rounded nose, which looked like a coffin. The car was only built for two years, as the Cord Corporation stopped manufacturing cars by the end of 1937.

NOT JUST ORNAMENTS

Radiator ornaments were an important styling feature on cars of the 1930s. A radiator holds water or a coolant that helps prevent the engine from overheating. The radiator ornament, which was fitted to the radiator cap, or cover, kept the coolant under pressure so that it worked properly. Ornaments were often decorative, and some companies hired professional artists to design them. Most ornaments were made of chrome, but some were made of crystal, others had little lights on them, and some moved with the wind. Thermometers, which told the driver the temperature the engine was running at, were even a part of some ornaments. By the late 1930s, the radiator was placed under the car's hood with the engine. Ornaments remained on top of the hood, purely as decoration, and became known as hood ornaments.

THE CLASSIC AUBURN

Auburns, also made by the Cord Corporation, were less expensive than Duesenbergs, and were produced in larger numbers. From 1928 to 1936, Auburns were known for their speed and sleek styling. Auburns were lower to the ground than many cars at the time, and had long, flowing **fenders**. Two-seater roadsters were popular models, along with supercharged **speedsters**. A supercharger is a device that forces more air into the engine, allowing a car to achieve faster speeds.

This 1933 Auburn speedster was also known as a boat-tail, because its back end looked like an upside down boat. This model was also powered by a 12-cylinder engine.

LINCOLN ZEPHYR

In 1936, Ford introduced the stylish Lincoln Zephyr. It was a beautiful car with graceful curves and flowing body lines. The Zephyr had rear fender skirts that covered most of the rear wheels for a smoother look. It was powered by a 12-cylinder engine. The body was of unitized construction, which means that the frame and the body was one piece. Up to this point, most car bodies were bolted onto the frame.

Several car manufacturers began building dream cars, such as this Y-Job made by GM, in the 1930s. Dream cars had very different styling that was meant to test the public's reaction. This determined if they should incorporate similar features on their production cars.

THE BIG THREE

By 1930 General Motors, Ford, and Chrysler were building more cars than any of the smaller companies. Good engineering, a reputation for reliability, styling, and a large number of dealers to service their cars helped them grow in size. They became known as the Big Three.

Ford, like General Motors and Chrysler, had many divisions that built cars to suit every person's pocket book. Lincoln, a division of Ford, built expensive luxury cars, such as this Zephyr.

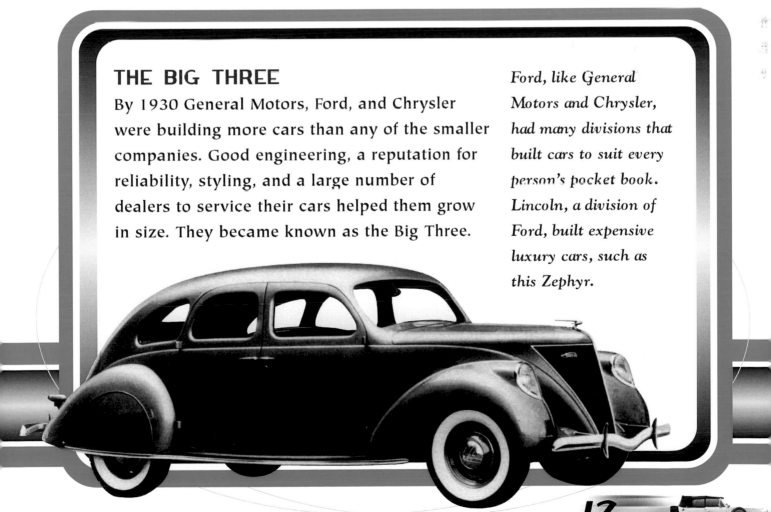

THE FORTIES

By the early 1940s, the Great Depression was over. People were back at work, and could afford to buy cars. World War II halted car production. Many car makers built vehicles and equipment for the war instead. Some of the technological improvements made during the war influenced car design.

THE ENVELOPE BODY

The styling of car bodies changed in the 1940s. A car's body and fenders began to flow together as one big shape. This shape enveloped the entire car and became known as the envelope body. The more rounded design did away with running boards, and the wheels were partially hidden by the fenders. Car trunks became larger because the back seat passengers now sat ahead of the rear wheels instead of on top of them. Car interiors were bigger, making for a more comfortable ride.

TRENDSETTERS

In 1938 Edsel Ford ordered a Lincoln Zephyr with a special body to drive during his winter vacation in Florida. He named his Lincoln the Continental, and its low, sleek styling caused a sensation everywhere he went. In 1940, the Continental became a production model. In 1941, General Motors debuted stylish Cadillacs with wide **grilles** that spread across the front of the cars and onto the front fenders. This feature was copied by car manufacturers worldwide.

The Lincoln Continental was originally supposed to be a one-of-a-kind car, but Edsel Ford decided to put the model into regular production in 1940.

TOUGH COMPETITION

Many of the smaller independent car manufacturers did not resume manufacturing automobiles after the war. Some companies switched their focus to products they had made during the war, such as Willys-Overland Motors, the manufacturer who made the Willys MB, otherwise known as the Jeep. Other manufacturers began making different items from farm and machine equipment to household appliances. Small car companies, such as Hudson, Packard, and Studebaker found it increasingly difficult to compete with the Big Three.

During World War II, many car manufacturers began making military equipment, such as airplanes and tanks. With many of the men at war, women were needed to work in factories.

These military trucks were shipped from the United States to Britain to help with the war effort.

POSTWAR AMERICA

After the war, there was a huge demand for cars in the United States. The pause in car production during the war meant that people were driving older cars, and were eager to buy newer models. Car manufacturers tried to keep up with demand but shortages of steel, rubber, and glass slowed down production.

A SHIFT IN SHIFTING

The transmission is the system of gears and other parts that engage the wheels to make a vehicle go faster or slower. Up until the 1940s, drivers shifted gears with a lever and **clutch**. During World War II, military tanks were equipped with a new type of transmission, called the Hydramatic transmission. The Hydramatic was an automatic transmission, as it did not require a clutch. This practical invention was incorporated into cars after the war. Drivers needed only to put their vehicles into "drive," and press on the gas pedal. The Hydramatic was instantly popular.

NEW AND IMPROVED!

After the war, there were few changes in car design, as manufacturers were too busy keeping up with demand to create new styles. It was not until 1949 that all-new designs appeared. Cars in the 1940s featured curved windshields, rather than flat glass. Wide, horizontal grilles and bright interior colors also became popular. One of the biggest style trends was introduced by Harley Earl, a designer at General Motors. He broke away from the traditional envelope body by adding **tail fins** to the 1948 Cadillac. His design was inspired by aircraft that were made during the war.

Due to focus on the war, many 1940s cars, such as this Lincoln Continental, were redesigned versions of earlier models.

Cars from Europe gave the Big Three a run for their money, such as this sporty 1948 MG TC convertible.

CARS FROM EUROPE

Following the war, young Americans fell in love with European sports cars. These foreign cars began arriving in U.S. showrooms in 1945. Many people liked how these smaller cars **handled**. The success of these models in North America helped European car manufacturers strengthen their businesses after the war. One of the most popular British models was the sporty MG.

The 1948 Tucker, by the Tucker Corporation, had a third headlight, known as the Cyclops Eye.

575 KIF
CALIFORNIA
TUCKER 1948

17

THE FIFTIES

Cars in the 1950s were bolder and brighter than ever before. People had money to spend, and this became obvious in the cars they bought. People splashed out on beautiful cars with vibrant colors and plenty of chrome trim. Tail fins became the hottest trend, and were featured on almost every model.

THE FABULOUS FIFTIES

By the 1950s, many automobiles came equipped with a heater, radio, better brakes, and automatic transmission. Car bodies were painted in two or three colors, a style known as two- or three-toning. Tail fins, made to look like the back ends of jets, gave cars a futuristic appeal. Hood ornaments became larger in the 1950s.

This 1957 Ford Thunderbird had the look of speed with its tail fins and hood scoop. Hood scoops are raised vents on cars' hoods. They bring cooler outside air into the engine, helping it to run better.

LAST OF THE INDEPENDENTS

Independent car manufacturers, such as Hudson, Nash, Studebaker, and Packard continued to sell cars into the 1950s, but they struggled to compete against the Big Three. General Motors, Chrysler, and Ford had more dealerships, and were able to offer more and newer models sooner than the independents. Most importantly, the Big Three could afford to sell their cars at lower prices than the independents. Many independents were forced to merge, or join together, to survive. Most of the independents, except for Hudson and Nash, which merged to form American Motors Corporation (AMC), disappeared by 1966.

TRACK RECORDS

In the 1950s, the sport of stock car racing became popular in the United States. Stock cars look similar to passenger cars, but they have special modifications, or changes, to them that allow for faster speeds. By the end of the decade, racing fans became interested in buying models that their favorite drivers raced at the track. Ford, Chrysler, and General Motors competed with each other to build the fastest cars with the most powerful engines. This was known as the horsepower race. Horsepower is a measurement of the power of an engine. In general, the higher the horsepower rating, the faster the cars can go.

(above) Wood-paneled station wagons were known as "woodie wagons" in the 1950s. They were associated with the surfers of California, as the extra length accommodated surf boards and other equipment.

(below) This 1958 Studebaker Commander has two-toning on its tail fins.

19

THE SIZZLING SIXTIES

In the 1960s, cars became more angular. Sporty muscle cars with powerful engines appealed to young racing enthusiasts, and many of them raced their own cars down abandoned airstrips and in other secluded areas. Foreign sports cars also continued to be popular.

THE SIZZLING SIXTIES

In the 1960s, American cars took on softer lines, flatter, sculpted sides, longer hoods, and shorter rear decks, or backseat passenger areas. The rear fenders swept up at the back higher than the front. The backs of the cars had a more chopped-off rear end. This was known as Coke bottle styling, named after the shape of the soft drink bottle. A sloping **fastback** roofline that stretched to the tip of the rear fenders was also popular.

THE MUSCLE CAR

Some of the biggest and most powerful engines ever built appeared in the 1960s. These engines were dropped into cars that became known as muscle cars. A muscle car is an American-made, mid-sized **coupe** built for speed. Muscle cars often featured bold racing stripes and special brand badges, or logos that were attached to the sides of the cars. They also featured stripped-down interiors to eliminate weight and allow cars to achieve greater speeds. Many muscle cars also had eye-catching wheels, and aggressive-looking, wide front grilles. Some had hood scoops, or vents in the hood to bring outside air into the engine compartment to help it run better.

Wide front grilles were known as "dollar grins" because they were so popular that any model that had them were guaranteed to sell quickly. This 1968 Dodge Charger also has bold striping at its tail.

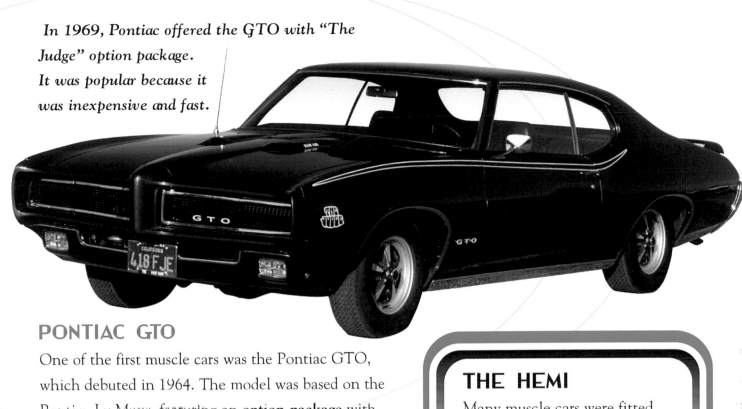

In 1969, Pontiac offered the GTO with "The Judge" option package. It was popular because it was inexpensive and fast.

PONTIAC GTO

One of the first muscle cars was the Pontiac GTO, which debuted in 1964. The model was based on the Pontiac Le Mans, featuring an **option package** with hood scoops, wide rear tires for better **traction**, heavy-duty suspension, and a powerful, **high-displacement** V8 engine. The GTO came as a convertible or **hardtop**, with several sporty features, including bucket seats and a **manual**, or hand-operated, transmission. It could accelerate from 0 to 60 miles per hour (97 kilometers per hour) in 7.2 seconds, which was very fast compared to most American cars at this time.

THE HEMI

Many muscle cars were fitted with Hemi engines. A Hemi has hemispherically shaped **cylinder heads**, rather than flat cylinder heads that are used in other engines. The hemispherical shape allows for more efficient burning of fuel.

Some of the most popular muscle cars are the SS models from Chevrolet. "SS" is short for Super Sport, which refers to the models' rigid suspensions.

21

This tiny MG convertible is suited to the sunny, warm climates of California and still sells well today.

BRITISH SPORTS CARS

The two-seater sports cars that started arriving in North America after World War II continued to be popular into the 1960s. Triumph, Austin-Healey, and Jaguar all produced attractive models, many of which are considered classics today. The body design in the 1960s was sleek and low to the ground.

MGB

British manufacturer MG produced many popular sports cars in the 1960s. In 1963, they debuted the MGB. It had a convertible top and wind-up windows. In 1965, the MGB GT hardtop appeared. It was not a fast sports car, but it was such a popular model that it was built until 1981, and is a favorite of classic car collectors today. *People who like sports cars love the distinctive body shape of an Austin 1-1 Healey.*

PONY CAR ROUNDUP

The 1960s saw pony cars rise to popularity. Pony cars are compact, speedy cars with large, powerful engines. The Ford Mustang, unveiled in 1964, is considered the first pony car. It had racing features, such as hood scoops and shiny chrome wheels, but it was not as expensive to purchase as a full-sized muscle car. The Mustang inspired other manufacturers to produce their own pony cars, such as the Chevrolet Camaro and the Pontiac Firebird. The Plymouth Barracuda was also a popular pony car.

This Ford Mustang is called a fastback, because the roof slopes straight down to the back tip of the car.

The Jaguar E-Type sports car was introduced in 1961. It featured a leather interior and wire wheels. The E-Type had superior performance, and could achieve up to 150 miles per hour (241 kilometers per hour). Aside from the coupe, it was also offered as an open two-seater.

THE SEVENTIES

Cars changed drastically in the 1970s. People became concerned about safety, insurance rates, and the rising costs of fuel. Safe and fuel-efficient vehicles became the order of the day.

KEEPING IT CLEAN

As the 1960s ended, people became more concerned about pollution and tried to adopt environmentally-conscious habits. New **emissions** standards were introduced, which forced car manufacturers to build engines that burned less fuel and created less air pollution. In 1973, the Organization of the Petroleum Exporting Countries (OPEC) launched an **embargo** against the United States, along with some other countries. The result of the embargo was that oil-producing countries in the **Middle East** began supplying much less oil to the United States. Since gasoline is made from oil, shortages of gasoline occurred. Gas-guzzling muscle cars were no longer practical, and many people became interested in smaller, fuel-efficient vehicles that would cost less to fill up.

During the 1973 oil embargo, gasoline shortages occurred across the country.

The Plymouth Barracuda was introduced in 1964. This "Cuda" was the 1970 model, the first to offer customers the choice of a Hemi engine.

SAFETY FIRST

While people became more concerned about air pollution, they also became more attentive to safety. Car manufacturers began designing cars with this in mind. Front seats were built with higher backs, to protect front passengers from neck injuries in the event of a crash. Bumpers were made larger, and with more rubber for added protection. Steering wheels were also made to be collapsible, so that drivers would not be rammed in the chest with the wheel in a crash. Dashboards were padded for the same reason.

LAST OF THE CLASSICS

Classic car enthusiasts generally agree that classic cars are vehicles that stand out from the others built around the same time. They are exceptional in performance or design, and in many cases, both. Some classic car enthusiasts consider the foreign sports cars and pony cars of the 1970s to be the last true classics. Others argue that innovations in design and technology are helping car manufacturers create new classics, and that it is only a matter of time before they are admired by classic car collectors worldwide.

By 1971, large cars with huge engines, such as this Chevelle, had become undesireable, as had the Hemi engine.

CLASSIC CARS TODAY

Classic cars do not roll off assembly lines at car manufacturing factories today. Despite this, classics are still seen on streets. Beautifully restored classics are also featured at auctions and rallies.

FROM RUST TO RICHES

Restoring classics is the process of fixing and cleaning up rusty, old classic cars. True classics are restored to look exactly as they did when they were brand new. Restoration can be very expensive, and may take years to complete just one car. Mechanical parts are often missing, so new ones have to be found or made by hand. Original paint color, carpets, and **upholstery** must be found, and all of the chrome must be made to look new.

SOLD, SOLD, SOLD!

Classic car auctions are places where people go to admire and purchase classic cars. During each auction, collectors may **bid** on vehicles they would like to purchase. Catalogs describe each car that is being offered for sale at the auction, so people can see what will be up for auction ahead of time. Images and descriptions of the cars are also featured on websites so that bidders from around the world can participate in the auction. Some buyers phone in their bids on specific cars.

Restoration is a very time-consuming and expensive process but it is usually worthwhile. Most restored classic cars are resold for several times their original price.

LET THE BIDDING BEGIN

At each auction, bidders are given a bidding card with a number on it so that the **auctioneer** can keep track of their bids. After a car is driven onto a staging area, the auctioneer begins by asking for a first bid at a certain amount of money. If nobody bids, the opening bid is lowered until someone holds up their bidding card. The bid may be raised by other bidders. The car goes to the highest bidder.

JOIN A CAR CLUB

Many classic car enthusiasts belong to car clubs. Members of classic car clubs meet regularly to discuss their cars, get help with locating parts, or share tips on restoring. Members of international clubs often communicate over the Internet. Some clubs are for specific car makes, such as the Studebaker Drivers Club, or the MG Car Club. Many classic car clubs organize rallies, in which people with a specific make of car drive their cars together, to show off their vehicles to the public.

(top) Classic Minis, which were originally made by BMW, await a rally through the countryside.

(above) Cars are often put on display before an auction so prospective buyers can look at them.

AUTOMOBILIA

Automobilia is a term that describes collectible classic car accessories, including hood ornaments and hub caps. It also includes books about classic cars, old advertising, and gas station items, such as station signs.

CAR BADGES

Car badges are metal logos that are attached to the sides of cars, often near the back. They are very popular among automotive enthusiasts. Some collectors have hundreds of badges of some of the oldest and rarest cars ever built. Original car badges are worth much more than new ones that are attached to modern cars.

MODELS AND DIE-CASTS

Some classic car enthusiasts collect models of their favorite classics. Model cars are small versions of the original cars. They are much cheaper than the full-sized versions. They also take up less room, fitting on a shelf rather than taking up an entire garage. Model cars are made of either plastic or metal. Metal models are called die-cast cars.

This building in New Hampshire displays automobilia, including old signs and gas pumps.

BIGGER TOYS

Pedal cars are toys that are made to look like real cars. Children can sit in them and move the pedals with their feet, like a bicycle. Pedal cars have been popular with children since around the 1920s. Some of the more expensive pedal cars at this time had small electric motors to help the driver go faster. There are pedal car clubs around the world. Some pedal cars are so rare that they cost as much as real cars.

(above) A young boy waves from his treasured pedal car, which was built in the 1930s.

AUTOMOTIVE MUSEUMS

Two of the most famous automobile museums in the United States are the National Automobile Museum in Reno, Nevada, and the Henry Ford Museum In Dearborn, Michigan. These museums house dozens of rare and one-of-a-kind dream cars. These museums attract classic car enthusiasts from around the world.

The Automotive Hall of Fame is another place to see old classic cars, such as this 1956 Cadillac.

BEHIND THE MACHINES

A number of car designers and stylists have created cars that changed the way automobiles would look for years to come.

HARLEY EARL

Harley Earl was born in 1893 in California. He was the son of coachbuilder J.W. Earl. In the 1920s, Harley Earl began working for General Motors to help design the 1927 LaSalle, and a year later the new Cadillac. Harley Earl was a leading designer with GM for three decades. He designed many stylish GM cars, including the futuristic Buick Y-Job, the Cadillac Eldorado and Chevrolet Corvette. He is also credited with being the first designer to put tail fins on cars. Earl retired as the head of styling at GM in 1958 and died in 1969.

GORDON MILLER BUEHRIG

Gordon Miller Buehrig was born in Illinois in 1904. He started his career in coachbuilding in 1921, and joined LeBaron in 1926. Beuhrig later went on to work for Packard, Stutz, GM, and Duesenberg, where he designed the coachwork for about half of the cars, as well as the beautiful hood ornament known as the Duesenbird. Buehrig also designed the Cord 810 in 1936. The styling of this car influenced many future designs from Lincoln, GM, and others. In 1951, the Cord 810 was named one of the eight best car designs of all time by the New York Museum of Fine Art.

One of Harley Earl's most memorable contributions to car design was his addition of tail fins to the Cadillac.

A woman poses with her Studebaker in the early 1950s.

RAYMOND LOEWY

Raymond Loewy was born in France in 1893, and immigrated to the United States in 1919. He was hired as a consultant for several small, independent car companies in the early 1930s. Loewy was hired by Studebaker in 1938. He had an eye for talent and surrounded himself with brilliant designers. The Loewy team helped design the 1947 Studebaker, as well as the bullet-nosed Studebaker Landcruiser of 1950. His Studebaker Coupe of 1953 won several awards in design. Raymond Loewy died in 1986.

DICK TEAGUE

Dick Teague was born in Los Angeles in 1923. In 1942, Teague became an illustrator at an aircraft company. There, he met a former General Motors stylist who encouraged him to take classes at the Art Center. Teague was hired by General Motors in 1948 to design headlights, hood ornaments, and other trim. In 1959, he joined American Motors Corporation (AMC), where he helped design the 1964 Rambler, the Marlin, the Gremlin, the Pacer, the AMX, and the Javelin. Teague became vice president of AMC until he retired in 1983. Teague died in 1991.

This antique gas pump would have been used by many classic cars when they were new to the road.

GLOSSARY

aluminum A metal

auctioneer Someone who requests bids for an item during an auction

bid A sum of money offered to buy something

clutch A device, controlled by a driver, that disengages the engine from the transmission while gears are shifted

coupe A two-door car

custom-built Built by hand

cylinder heads The tops of cylinders in an engine

cylinders The chambers in an engine where pistons pump up and down

embargo An official agreement to stop trading with a particular nation

emissions Fumes from fuel that pollute the air

fastback A car with a roof that slopes in a straight line to the back of the car

fenders Guards around car wheels, which prevent mud from splashing up

grilles Metal grating at the front of a vehicle that allows air to circulate to the radiator

handled How a car took corners and managed bumps in the road, and how well a driver was able to control it

hardtop A car with a hard roof. Some hardtops are removable

high-displacement A powerful engine that pulls large amounts of fuel and air into its chambers

investing Giving money to a company in the hopes that a profit will be made

Middle East The countries that border the southern and eastern shores of the Mediterranean Sea

obsolete No longer made

option package A set of features that a driver can add to a car for extra cost

radiator A device that helps cool an engine

restored Made something like brand new

showrooms Where cars are displayed for sale

speedsters Cars that are made to go fast

stocks Shares, often in the form of certificates, which represent owning a portion of a company, and entitling the owner to a part of a company's profits, or earnings

suspensions Systems of springs and shock absorbers that help cars handle bumps in the road so that passengers are not jostled

tail fins Pieces of bodywork that extend from the back of a car

traction Pulling action of an object over a surface

upholstery Fabric that covers seating

World War II A global conflict that occurred between 1939 and 1945

INDEX